TECUMSEH

By Anne Schraff

DILLON PRESS, INC.
MINNEAPOLIS, MINNESOTA

Dillon Press, Inc., 500 South Third Street
Minneapolis, Minnesota 55415

Printed in the United States of America

Library of Congress Cataloging in Publication Data

Schraff, Anne E.
  Tecumseh.

  (The Story of an American Indian)
  SUMMARY: A biography of the Shawnee warrior, orator,
and leader who united a confederacy of Indians in an effort
to save Indian land from the advance of white soldiers and
settlers.
  1. Tecumseh, Shawnee chief (1768-1813—Juvenile literature. 2. Shawnee Indians—Biography—Juvenile literature.
3. Indians of North America—Ohio Valley—Biography—
Juvenile literature. [1. Tecumseh, Shawnee chief, 1768 1813.
2. Shawnee Indians—Biography. 3. Indians of North America
—Biography] I. Title.
E99.S35T32   970'.004'97 [B]   78 13956
ISBN 0-87518-166-X

TECUMSEH

In 1812 warriors from thirty-two American Indian tribes,
ranging from Canada to the Gulf of Mexico, fought
under the banner of Tecumseh's Indian confederacy.
His leadership had put together the greatest union
of Indian forces ever assembled in a last effort to save
Indian land from the onslaught of white soldiers and
settlers. As an orator, military strategist, and leader of
his Shawnee people, Tecumseh has few equals. He
has been called one of our great American leaders.

This map shows the places and events that are important to Tecumseh's story.

Contents

Everyone in the Shawnee village looked skyward at a strange and beautiful sight.

CHAPTER I

A Sign
from Heaven

The chilly night was bright with stars. An early spring covered the hills with tender grass. The scent of phlox filled the air, and the wind whispered through the wild plum trees. Suddenly, everyone in the Shawnee village looked skyward at a strange and beautiful sight. A great meteor came from the north and for a few moments streaked across the moonless sky. The Shawnee had never seen anything so bright. Many saw it as a sign that a great event had happened.

Moments after the meteor disappeared, the strong, healthy cry of a newborn child filled the night. Tecumseh, the Indian leader, had been born. For the Shawnee, the appearance of the meteor and the birth of Tecumseh were to be forever linked together.

Tecumseh has been called one of our great American leaders. As an orator, or public speaker, he has been ranked with Patrick Henry. As a military leader he has been compared with Ulysses S. Grant and William T. Sherman. He was called a genius by the American general who opposed him in battle, William Henry Harrison.

On the night of his birth, Tecumseh's father, the Shawnee Puckeshinwa, found his wife lying on a buffalo robe. She held the newborn baby tenderly in her arms. Methoataske, Tecumseh's mother, was of the Creek people. Her name meant turtle-laying-her-eggs-in-the-sand, a tribute to her many strong children.

The new parents had no trouble naming the baby. According to Shawnee custom, the children were named according to an *unsoma,* or special event. This important event occurred within ten days of the child's birth. In the case of the newborn child, the sign came at the time he was born. Thus he was called Tecumseh, which means "a great spirit going south" or "I cross somebody's path." The Shawnee believed that *Moneto,* or God, intended great things for this unusual child.

Tecumseh was born in 1768 in the Shawnee village of Old Piqua, a village of four thousand people located near what is now the city of Springfield, Ohio. The wood-frame homes of the village, called *wegiwas,* spread for miles along the west bank of the Mad River, a gentle waterway rich in fish. Along the banks wild game was plentiful. Cornstalk, the tribal chief of the Shawnee, ruled the village from his home on the Scioto River to the east.

It would be hard to imagine a finer home for the Shawnee than Old Piqua. The rich riverbottom soil was so fertile that fish did not have to be planted with seeds to insure a good crop. Using tools made from bison bones and turtle shells, the people plowed the soft earth. The Shawnee raised beans, melons, and corn. Their favorite foods were bear ribs, root jelly, hominy, corn cakes, and succotash. Sweet spring water bubbled from nearby springs. The Shawnee believed that *Moneto* had given them this beautiful and generous land because he loved them.

The Shawnee people were wanderers—moving, dividing, and coming together all over what is now the eastern United States. Their original home was most likely in the area we know as Ohio. From there they drifted south into Kentucky and Tennessee. At one time they lived in lands that now form part of fifteen different states.

In their travels the Shawnee did not move together in large groups. Instead, small bands of families went from place to place along the rivers. A handsome and intelligent people, the Shawnee were highly respected by other American Indian tribes. They were noted as fine woodsmen, good hunters, and a practical and high-spirited people.

Of the many ceremonies of the Shawnee, the Green Corn Feast was the most important. This happy time marked the

This museum display shows what the Feast of the Green Corn might have looked like.

beginning of each new year. Houses and clothing were cleaned, and broken articles were thrown out. All arguments were settled, and debts were paid. Wrongdoers were forgiven, and people sent into exile could now return.

Just before the ceremony began, the men fasted and drank a strong tea known as the Black Drink. The tea was tar black in color and brewed from hollylike leaves. It was drunk hot from a gourd and was supposed to purify their bodies.

During the ceremony, four sticks were laid on the ground, each pointing to one of the four winds. Across the sticks were laid four ears of green corn. A new fire was struck because all of the old fires had been put out. From the new fire, every woman would rekindle her own house fire.

All the Shawnee children listened with awe to the tales the elders told. Much of the storytelling concerned the early history of the Shawnee. The saddest tales were about contacts between the Shawnee people and the Europeans. One of the first meetings took place in the 1530s, when the French explorer, Jacques Cartier, reached the Gulf of St. Lawrence.

It was a Shawnee, Nika, who guided LaSalle on his exploration of the Ohio River. He was a companion to LaSalle for many years, even taking trips to France. The Shawnee got along well with the French because they came to trade, unlike the English, who came to settle the land.

In the 1750s, trouble came to the Shawnee because the English began pushing many eastern tribes westward. Conflicts arose among the Indians who lost their lands and tried to settle on the land of other tribes. During this time

Tecumseh grew up in the beautiful land of the Ohio Valley.

the French and English fought for control of the New World, and the French lost. The Shawnee had been allies of the French, so they lost as well. By the time of Tecumseh's birth, the Shawnee had to deal with the many new settlers who came to take their land.

Tecumseh showed signs of leadership as a small boy. Other children, even those who were older, followed his lead. He was so skilled at games that all the other boys wanted to be on his side during the contests. An unusually tall and very handsome child, he loved sports and enjoyed running among the poplars, elms, and chestnuts of Old Piqua.

For the first six years of Tecumseh's life, his life centered around his mother. Methoataske was a strong-minded woman who spoke beautifully. Tecumseh loved to listen to his mother's fine voice and marvelous words. In this way he learned much about the power of words and the art of speech. Methoataske taught her son a deep distrust for the white people. When she was a small child, she had heard tales of how the whites had mistreated her people. She told all this to her son.

The great leader, Cornstalk, came to visit Old Piqua when Tecumseh was six. As Cornstalk spoke to the Shawnee, no child listened with such attention as Tecumseh. Cornstalk became the first real hero in the small boy's life. From the words of the Shawnee chief as he described his battles with the white invaders, Tecumseh learned the danger of the strange settlers.

As the land-hungry whites moved ever westward, the Shawnee were fighting to keep their land. The white settlers believed that all the Indians should be shoved aside and the entire area opened for claims. A white trapper killed an Indian man and woman for stealing his dog. Soon after, a dozen Shawnee were killed in a raid by whites. It wasn't long before land speculators were pushing for open warfare. Settlers attacked Shawnee villages and hunting parties, and war raged along the entire frontier.

Young Tecumseh found out how dangerous the white people could be. His father was a strong supporter of Cornstalk and fought with the Shawnee leader in battles against the whites. One day Puckeshinwa had a strong feeling that he would soon die. He called his eldest son, Cheeseekau, to his side and made him promise to take care of the younger children if anything should happen to their father. Then Puckeshinwa went into battle.

The Shawnee lost the Battle of Point Pleasant, and shortly afterward Puckeshinwa lost his life. On his way home, he was stopped by white hunters, who wanted him to guide them through the forest. He saw blood on their hands and thought they had just come from fighting the Shawnee. Angered, he refused to help them.

Never before had the leader of the hunting party been insulted by an Indian. He drew his pistol and shot Puckeshinwa in the chest. Leaving him to die alone, the hunters rode away into the forest.

In Old Piqua Methoataske searched the horizon for some sign of her husband. She would soon give birth to another child, but she knew that she must go out and look for Puckeshinwa. He might be in desperate need of help.

Methoataske and Tecumseh searched the woods in the darkness. Finally they found Puckeshinwa, near death but still able to tell what had happened to him. As the boy listened to his father's last words, all the tales he had heard against the white people came to life.

Tecumseh watched his mother kneel down beside Puckeshinwa. He heard her cry out in pain and grief. The distrust that Methoataske had always felt for the whites now deepened into hatred. She told Tecumseh that he must become a warrior and avenge the death of his father.

Tecumseh helped carry his father's body back to a place beside the Mad River. Again, during the funeral, Methoataske cried out against the white people. The small boy never forgot the bitter words of his mother. No more would Tecumseh run carefree in the shadow of the chestnut tree.

CHAPTER II

Fire and
Ashes

Soon after the death of Puckeshinwa, Methoa-taske gave birth to her last child, a boy named Laulewasika. She looked to her son Cheeseekau to carry out the will of his father by helping to raise the younger children.

There was much for Cheeseekau to teach young Tecumseh. Before long a great love and respect grew between the brothers. From Cheeseekau Tecumseh learned the traditions, laws, and skills of the Shawnee. Since their people had no written language, all lessons had to be passed down through stories and personal example. In Tecumseh's case, the lessons would be passed from older to younger brother.

To survive in the forest, a young Shawnee had to become a skilled hunter. Soon Tecumseh came to know the tracks made by the different animals. The fox made small circular tracks, and the thin toes of the raccoon could be easily told from the smaller prints of the opossum and muskrat. Tecumseh learned how to build traps and deadfalls. He learned the use of the bow and arrow so well that he could shoot accurately from a fast horse.

Cheeseekau took Tecumseh fishing and exploring in the rivers and forests. Patiently, the older boy pointed out which roots were safe to eat and which could be used for

From Cheeseekau Tecumseh learned to hunt the animals of the forest.

medicines. Tecumseh found such tasty foods as wild strawberries, blueberries, hazelnuts, wild apples, and grapes. He learned the names and uses for everything in the land near his home.

Blackfish, the chief of Old Chillicothe, a Shawnee village south of Old Piqua, acted as a foster father for Tecumseh. Blackfish guided Tecumseh in the search for his *pawawka*. This was an object of spiritual value through which a Shawnee received the blessings of *Moneto*. He also taught Tecumseh his methods of warfare, stressing hit-and-run raids and the importance of surprising the enemy. Tecumseh learned that a leader is never defeated until he has given up in his own heart. As he grew older, he came to know the value of all that Blackfish had taught him.

Tecumseh's older sister, Tecumapease, also took part in his upbringing. From her he learned to be kind to people and animals. She taught him to share what he had with the other members of the tribe, most of all those who could not provide for themselves. Tecumseh learned to respect the Shawnee way of life and to judge his actions by the laws and traditions of his people.

As he grew up, Tecumseh began to show a special concern for the aged in his tribe. When winter approached, he would travel through Old Piqua and Old Chillicothe to see if all the old people had weatherproof homes. If he found a *wegiwa* battered and torn, he would repair it.

Tecumseh brought skins to the aged Shawnee so they could make warm clothing for the winters. While hunting, he would save a portion and bring it to those too old or sick to hunt for themselves. In sharing his goods, Tecumseh did not choose those who held a high social position in his tribe. Often he would give the best of the game he had hunted to the poorest Shawnee. For Tecumseh, however, the peaceful days of hunting and sharing with his people would not last for long.

Just three years after the death of his father, Tecumseh's hero Cornstalk was killed by whites in a way that shocked many people living on the frontier. It happened at the time the Americans were fighting the British during the Revolutionary War. Both sides tried to gain allies among the Indian tribes, and the Americans asked Cornstalk to come to Fort Randolph to help draw some maps.

Cornstalk urged the Shawnee not to take sides in the war, but he agreed to come to Fort Randolph with his son

As a boy Tecumseh admired the great Shawnee leader, Cornstalk. The young boy was saddened when Cornstalk was killed by white soldiers.

Ellinipsico and a small party of warriors. About the same time, a white man named Gilmore was killed while hunting with friends along the Ohio River. Indians were blamed, and someone remembered seeing Cornstalk and his party in the area on the day of the killing.

In anger, a group of white soldiers at the fort decided that someone in Cornstalk's party had killed Gilmore. When they went to the cabin where the Indians were staying, Cornstalk bravely opened the door. At once the whites opened fire. Ellinipsico was shot to death as he knelt beside his dying father. The other Shawnee tried to escape, but they were surrounded and killed, too. Young Tecumseh had learned another bitter lesson.

After the murder of Cornstalk, the conflict on the frontier grew more and more violent. In the battles between the Americans and the English, most Indian tribes sided with the English. An American army, commanded by General George Rogers Clark, was sent to defeat the Indians on the western frontier. Part of his strategy was to burn down Shawnee villages and destroy crops.

Old Piqua was in the midst of one of the finest growing seasons in years. Five hundred acres of corn had been planted, and the ears were nearly ready for harvest. Pumpkins, beans, and squash were full and plentiful. With one thousand men, Clark marched on Old Chillicothe and burned the town to the ground. Word spread that he was heading for Old Piqua. Tecumseh saw terror in the eyes of his people. The beautiful town that he had known all his life was in great danger.

When the American army arrived, cannon fired on the wood-frame *wegiwas* of Old Piqua. The Shawnee warriors fought bravely, but they were no match for the rifles and cannons of the white soldiers. People ran from the flames that quickly destroyed the village homes and all the corn in the fields. Using rifle butts, the soldiers smashed the pumpkins and ripped loose the beans and squash. For three miles along the Mad River where Old Piqua had once stood, nothing remained but charred ruins and scattered ashes.

At night in the forest, Tecumseh listened helplessly to the cries of his people burying their dead. The Shawnee who survived built a new town called Piqua on the banks of the Miami River. To the Shawnee, "Piqua" means a "town that rises from the ashes."

Tecumseh struggled to deal with the hatred for the whites that was growing within him. By nature he was kindly and generous, but everything seemed to prove what his mother had told him as a small boy. Now he had to avenge not only the death of his father and Cornstalk, but the burning of Old Piqua as well.

Again, shortly after the end of the Revolutionary War, an American army under General Clark came to Shawnee land. This time the Shawnee did not try to do battle with Clark's army, but they carried out many hit-and-run raids against smaller groups of soldiers.

Tecumseh went for the first time as a warrior on one of these raids. Traveling in a war party with his brother Cheeseekau, he attacked a group of American soldiers on the Mad River. In the first moments Cheeseekau was wounded. Gunfire exploded like thunder around Tecumseh. Terror stricken, he abandoned his companions and fled from the fighting.

Among the Shawnee, it was the custom to let wrongdoers punish themselves for their misdeeds. At nightfall in the Shawnee village, the fires were lit as usual. The warriors spoke of the day's battle, and those who had performed with courage were praised. Nothing at all was said about Tecumseh. In his own heart he suffered the shame and guilt of his fear.

Tecumseh was never again to run from battle. From that day on, no warrior left the battlefield after him. Even if he stood alone, he remained to fight until the battle was over.

With the end of the Revolutionary War, more and more white settlers came to settle on Shawnee land. For the American Indians on the frontier, every white settlement marked another step toward the loss of their homeland. The Shawnee often attacked riverboat traffic because it

The white settlers came down the Ohio River to settle on Shawnee land.

brought supplies to the white settlements. If they could stop the flow of supplies, they believed they could force the whites to leave their land.

Tecumseh proved himself as a warrior and leader on one of these attacks. He was traveling in a Shawnee war party along the Ohio River. When two flatboats appeared, the war party planned an ambush. After a furious battle in which Tecumseh fought bravely, all but one of the whites were killed.

The white prisoner was taken by Tecumseh's companions, bound to a stake, and burned alive. Tecumseh watched in horror. For the rest of his life, he would never forget the cries of the dying man. At last he stepped forward before his companions, his face dark with rage. Most of the men with him were twice or three times his age. In spite of his great respect for his elders, he began to condemn them for what they had done to the prisoner. He told them he was ashamed of his Shawnee brothers. He said they had done an evil thing and were not worthy in the eyes of *Moneto*.

In the ranks of the warriors, there was silence. A boy not yet sixteen was telling full-grown men how to behave. Tecumseh was turning their triumph into an act of shame.

Cheeseekau stepped alongside his brother. He agreed with what Tecumseh had said, and he blamed himself for having lacked the courage to speak out as his younger brother had done.

Never again, before the eyes of Tecumseh, would a prisoner be tortured. In many future battles, the lives of the prisoners would be saved by the simple fact of someone saying, "Tecumseh is here."

CHAPTER III

A Lost Homeland

When Tecumseh was nineteen, he went with Cheeseekau on a long hunting trip through what is now Ohio and south to the Tennessee River. The two brothers spent months together exploring the forests and hunting buffalo and deer. It was one of the happiest times in Tecumseh's life.

Tecumseh was proud of being a good hunter, and he liked to compete with his friends. Once he made a bet with them that he could bring down more deer during three days than any of the others. At the end of the three days, the other young men had each killed twelve deer. Tecumseh had brought down thirty deer. As usual, he gave the meat and skins to those in need. Because of Tecumseh's kindness, the coming winter would be easier for many Indian families.

During this hunting trip Tecumseh had a serious accident. He and Cheeseekau were chasing buffalo on mustangs. The mustang Tecumseh was riding stumbled, and he was thrown to the ground. He was badly hurt, breaking his leg in at least one place. It took several months for Tecumseh to recover from the injury. This was the last time he would spend a long period of his life hunting and exploring freely. Tecumseh had become a young warrior, and he was needed

Tecumseh fell from his mustang and badly injured himself while chasing buffalo on a hunting trip.

by his people to defend their homeland.

As more and more white people came looking for land, warfare between the Shawnee and the settlers became a constant series of raids and counter raids. The Shawnee felt that the lands north of the Ohio River should belong to the Indians. The whites should stay south and east of the river. The settlers, however, did not agree. Each year more of them came to claim the fine farmland north of the Ohio.

Tecumseh, Cheeseekau, and the other Shawnee warriors attacked the new frontier settlements. They hoped that such attacks would keep the whites from settling north of the Ohio. But the Shawnee did not know how many thousands of white farmers were determined to settle on their land.

Tecumseh traveled with his brother in a small group of

warriors. True to Shawnee tradition, the war party ranged far and wide on their raiding trips. One night Tecumseh and his friends were camped on the Tennessee River. They had been hunting, and now they were dressing the meat around the campfire.

Suddenly Tecumseh saw shadows in the woods. Years of careful training by Cheesekau made him alert to the slightest sign of trouble. He knew by the number of shadows that there were many men around the camp. Tecumseh kept speaking in a normal voice. He did not want the whites to attack right away. He told the Shawnee that they were surrounded and he would tell them what to do. They should sit quietly and pretend that nothing was wrong. Tecumseh got up slowly and acted as if he was straightening his buffalo robe. Then he flung the robe over the fire, darkening the camp.

The white men attacked, but they couldn't see the Shawnee anymore. Tecumseh led his companions in a charge through the confused whites, who were so startled by the sudden turn of events that they shot wildly in all directions. The Shawnee raced into the woods, circled around the camp, and attacked the whites from behind. By this time the white men thought the woods were full of Indian warriors. Several whites were killed in the fighting, but no Shawnee fell. After the battle many Shawnee warriors looked to Tecumseh to lead them.

Shawnee war parties were fighting with the Creek and Cherokee people against the white settlers near the new frontier settlement of Nashville. The combined Indian forces had captured a place called Ziegler's Station and were planning an attack on John Buchanan's Station, a fort four miles south of the white town. On the night before the attack, Cheeseekau told the Shawnee warriors that he had a vision of his death in the battle to come.

The Indian forces attacked the fort in the pre-dawn darkness. Cheeseekau climbed the blockade fence and tried to set fire to the buildings. As soon as he reached the top of the fence, he was wounded by gunfire. Cheeseekau shouted to the other warriors to keep fighting. Once more he tried to set fire to the buildings. He was shot again and lay still. Tecumseh watched his brother die. That night he carried Cheeseekau's body to a secret place in the forest where he buried him.

The Indians lost the battle of Buchanan's Station. Afterward the Shawnee warriors in the south held a council and chose Tecumseh to be their leader. By this time his fame as a warrior had spread to many Indian tribes. Tecumseh devoted his life to stopping the white invaders and saving the land of his people.

Other Indian leaders, such as Joseph Brant, had come to believe that only through combining their forces could they hope to defend their land from the whites. The Miami chief, Little Turtle, had already shown that they could do so. Using the warriors of allied tribes, he had defeated two American armies. The U.S. government feared his strength. They chose General Anthony Wayne, a revolutionary war hero, to lead a new campaign against the Indians. During the winter of 1793-94, Wayne trained his soldiers for the difficult fight ahead.

Tecumseh, now a strong young man of twenty-five, acted as the leader of the Indian scouts. As a young warrior he had fought under Little Turtle in the two Indian victories.

He had won respect for his able and fearless leadership under fire, and the older Indian chiefs placed great trust in him.

This time, however, the Indian leaders could not agree among themselves. Little Turtle spoke against a large-scale battle with the American army because he did not believe the Indians could win. They were greatly outnumbered by the Americans, who had been well-trained and equipped with guns, bayonets, and horses. Blue Jacket, the Shawnee chief, spoke strongly for fighting the Americans. The Indians had beaten them before, he said, and they could do it again. In the end they followed Blue Jacket's advice.

Outnumbered and outgunned by the American army, the Indian forces lost the Battle of Fallen Timbers.

On August 20, 1794, the two forces met along the Mau-mee River in a large clearing among a tangle of fallen trees. Throughout the battle, Tecumseh fought wherever the action was most desperate, rallying the warriors again and again. Wayne's sharpshooters kept most of the Indians pinned down. His cavalry charged at the Indians from all sides. The American infantry attacked in a close-packed line with their bayonets, scattering the warriors. Soon the battle was over. Tecumseh led a final charge and captured one of the American field guns, but finally he had to retreat with the rest of the warriors.

In the treaty that followed the Battle of Fallen Timbers,

The Shawnees had to give up much of their land in the treaty that followed the battle. Tecumseh had learned another sad lesson.

the Indians were forced to give up much of their land in what is now Ohio. The land given up included Old Piqua, Old Chillicothe, Piqua, and most of the Shawnee homeland. Tecumseh refused to attend the treaty council and did not sign what became known as the Treaty of Greenville.

He had learned a sad lesson during the battle. He was a brave and clever leader, but the white leader had been clever, too. In the battles that lay ahead, the Shawnee would need a leader who could unite all the Indian tribes in the war against the whites. Tecumseh saw such a union as the Indian's only hope. And he would come to believe that he could unite and lead them.

CHAPTER IV

Chief of the Beautiful River

After the Battle of Fallen Timbers, many young warriors of the Indian tribes in the Ohio Valley looked to Tecumseh to lead them. No longer was he just a Shawnee leader. He became known as the "chief of the beautiful river," an Indian name for the Ohio River. Indians of many tribes respected Tecumseh because he refused to recognize the Treaty of Greenville. He said that no single Indian tribe had the right to sell land that was given to all the Indian people by the Great Spirit.

Tecumseh lived among the Shawnee for several years after the treaty. During this time relations between the whites and the Indians were peaceful, even though many new settlers came to the Ohio Valley looking for farmland. Tecumseh began to build up a group of devoted followers from several tribes. He lived simply and did not drink and gamble as many Indians did who came in contact with white traders and settlers.

When Tecumseh was twenty-eight-years old, his people asked him when he would marry. Among the Shawnee, all men and women were expected to marry and have children. Since the Shawnee had few people compared to other tribes, every child born was important to their survival.

In the Shawnee village there was a woman named Manete who needed a husband. She was older than Tecumseh and he did not love her, but he married her to fulfill his duty to his people. Manete bore one child, a son named Puge-shashenwa.

After his son was born, Tecumseh gave Manete many gifts of meat and skins, and she returned to the home of her father. Among the Shawnee, this meant that the marriage had ended. Manete had a son now, and she was happier living with him and with her father. As the child grew, Tecumseh's sister Tecumapease helped to bring him up. She taught him many of the things she had taught Tecumseh when he was a boy.

Discouraged by the many whites who settled on Shawnee land, Tecumseh moved with his followers to the White River in what is now Indiana. He came back from time to time to visit his son and to attend councils of tribal leaders. First in the councils of the Shawnee, and then in the councils of Indians and whites in the Ohio Valley, Tecumseh became known as an orator, or public speaker. Though he did not accept the Treaty of Greenville, he acted to maintain peace between Indians and whites when it seemed that war might break out.

When a white man named Thomas Herrod was killed. near Old Chillicothe, the settlers believed that a Shawnee had done it. They demanded that the guilty Indian be turned over to them. This did not happen, and the angry settlers attacked innocent Shawnee. The Shawnee struck back by attacking white settlements. It looked as if Indians and whites might soon go to war.

A group of settlers asked Tecumseh to speak at a meeting

Because of the many white settlers who came to Shawnee land, Tecumseh moved with his followers to what is now Indiana.

of the whites and Shawnee in the area. When Tecumseh spoke, a hushed silence spread over the crowd. He told everyone to calm down. The Shawnee wanted to live in peace on their land, he said, and both sides should stop attacking each other. Tecumseh always spoke in the Shawnee language in public speeches, but his words affected

Indians and whites alike. Those who heard him would never forget his powerful voice and total command of an audience. An American general who once heard Tecumseh speak said, "I have heard many great orators, but I never saw one with the vocal powers of Tecumseh." Because Tecumseh's word was respected by the whites and the Shawnee, war did not break out over the death of Thomas Herrod.

Tecumseh's power of speech came from many sources. Methoataske was a fine speaker, and Tecumapease had taught him the highest ideals of the Shawnee. As a boy, Tecumseh had listened to the beautiful words of Cornstalk and Joseph Brant. He had such a fine memory that he could recall every word of the Treaty of Greenville. Another source was the brief friendship he had with a young white woman.

One day while hunting in the forest, Tecumseh met a tough Irishman named Galloway. Galloway lived with his daughter in a cabin near Old Chillicothe. He was not at all what one might call a typical white settler. For one thing, he enjoyed books and had brought hundreds of them to his frontier home. He liked the wilderness and wanted to leave the forest and the wild animals alone. Most white settlers wanted to tear down the trees and build barns and fences. Soon Tecumseh and Galloway became good friends, and the young Indian leader became a frequent visitor to the Galloway cabin. There he met his friend's daughter, Rebecca.

Rebecca liked Tecumseh the first time he came to the Galloway home. Attractive and intelligent, she had read all of the books in her father's cabin. Tecumseh knew some

English from the white people he had met. With his quick mind, he soon learned what Rebecca taught him of her language so that they could speak easily with each other.

Rebecca read to Tecumseh from the Bible, history books, and the plays of Shakespeare. He listened closely to the stories of other warriors from history. Later Tecumseh would surprise white audiences by talking about the life of Jesus or the battles of Alexander the Great. But now he was not so much interested in learning as in listening to Rebecca.

Tecumseh fell in love with Rebecca. Each time he came to visit her, he brought her special gifts. She especially liked a large silver comb for her blond hair. When he arrived one day in a birchbark canoe, the young couple paddled down the river to a place under the trees. There they sat for hours, talking and sharing ideas. Tecumseh called Rebecca the Star of the Lake. Before long he asked her father for her hand in marriage.

Galloway respected Tecumseh and would have been happy to have him as a son-in-law. In fact, the old Irishman liked Tecumseh much better than the settlers who had courted Rebecca. Galloway told Tecumseh to ask Rebecca herself. If she said yes, then he would give his approval.

Tecumseh asked Rebecca to marry him. She accepted on one important condition. He must leave the Shawnee and live as a white man. He must give up the ways of his people, for she would not become an Indian wife.

Tecumseh was proud of being a Shawnee. He did not want to live as a white man, even if that were possible. Many of the whites he knew killed Indian people for no reason. And it was the whites who had killed his father and brother

William Henry Harrison wanted the Indians in the Ohio Valley to move west to the other side of the Mississippi River.

and burned his village.

Above all, Tecumseh did not like what happened to Indians who lived in close contact with whites. White traders and settlers gave Indians whiskey to turn them into drunkards. That way they would not cause trouble to the settlers who came to take their land. Indians who did not drink whiskey often died from diseases such as smallpox that the settlers brought with them.

Sadly, Tecumseh told Rebecca that he was born a Shawnee and would die as one of his people. Even though he loved her, he would not try to live as a white man. So Tecumseh left Rebecca and never saw her again.

From this time on, Tecumseh put all his efforts into his dream of uniting the Indian tribes. He dreamed of a wilderness that would last forever. Wild animals would run free amid thick forests and sparkling rivers. The people would hunt what they needed and no more. They would live as they had done for thousands of years before the coming of the whites.

Another young man had a different dream for Tecumseh's homeland. William Henry Harrison, the new governor of the Indiana Territory, had a vision of many thousands of white farmers building barns and houses. He dreamed of neat fences, thriving crops, and busy cities. To open up the land to the white farmers, Harrison wanted to force the Indians to leave their lands and move to the other side of the Mississippi River. Few white people had been there, and many thought of it as a barren place where the Indians could be sent and forgotten.

From 1795 to 1812, there was a great westward movement of white settlers. Overcrowding, high taxes, and poor soil caused them to leave New England and the Middle Atlantic states. New roads were built into the Ohio Valley. Most of these roads ended up in the heart of Shawnee country.

Land speculators helped lure people into the Ohio Valley. In 1800, a white farmer could buy hundreds of acres for two dollars per acre. Tecumseh and his friends watched in anger as land offices sprang up all over Shawnee country. Every day more whites came.

The settlers did not mind taking the land from the Indians. Many of them looked at American Indians as no different from wild animals which had to be pushed aside. Their view of the Indians was shared to some extent by officials in the state and federal governments of the United States.

President Thomas Jefferson said that the Indians could no longer follow their way of life. Either they would have to move to the lands beyond the Mississippi River that the whites didn't want, or they would have to settle in one place and live like the whites.

Jefferson set up a system of land agents to visit Indian tribes and persuade their leaders to sell Indian land. The agents would try to get the Indian leaders to sign away their land in treaties. For most of the agents, it did not matter what method they used to buy the land. Often whiskey, gifts, and other bribes proved difficult for Indian leaders to resist.

In 1802 William Henry Harrison called chiefs from the Kickapoo, Wea, and Delaware tribes to a council at Vincennes, the capital of the Indiana Territory. Harrison told the chiefs that they must sign a treaty selling most of their land. When the chiefs refused, Harrison told them the whites would take the land by force if they didn't sign the treaty. For days he bribed and threatened them. Finally they signed.

In treaties such as this one, American Indians were losing their lands in the Ohio Valley and in other areas all over the country. Tecumseh bitterly opposed the treaties, but alone he could not fight them. He knew that his dream of a strong union of Indian tribes was more urgent than ever.

CHAPTER V

The Prophet's
Magic

In 1805 the younger brother of Tecumseh, Laulewasika, became well known as a religious leader among the
Shawnee. As a young man he had turned to whiskey and
seemed to have no real purpose in life. He had been thought
of as a lazy drunkard who was a disgrace to his family and
his people. All this changed when he went through a sudden
religious awakening.

Laulewasika had a vision in which he saw heaven and
hell. He said he was taken up into the clouds and shown
the happiness of heaven. There the people were sober,
pure, and peace loving. He was also shown the dwelling
place of the devil. There he saw many drunkards with fire
coming out of their mouths. According to Laulewasika,
these people had been sent to hell because they died as
drunkards. They would never see heaven.

Laulewasika changed his name to Tenskwatawa, which
means "the open door." He said he would open a new door
for the Shawnee people and teach them a better way of life.
From this time on he was known as the Prophet.

Tecumseh was pleased with the new purpose in his brother's life and strongly believed in the moral code that the
Prophet began to teach. According to the code, all Indians

should live together in peace on the land that was given to them by the Great Spirit. They should not drink liquor, and they should share everything the Great Spirit had given them equally among themselves. The aged and the sick should be respected and cared for, and men and women should have equal rights and duties. Indians should not live together with whites because their strength lay in the peaceful union of their own people. In many ways the code re-

The Prophet asked all Indians to unite and to return to the old way of life.

flected the traditional laws and values of the Shawnee.

The Prophet's message and Tecumseh's dream of an Indian union were very much alike. Tecumseh answered his brother's call to build a settlement open to Indians of all tribes at the place where the Treaty of Greenville was signed. Here the Prophet's code was put into effect. The people worked hard, raised their crops, and shared among themselves. No one drank whiskey.

Governor Harrison worried about the Greenville settlement and about the Indians who came to live there. He feared that the religious influence of the Prophet would spread to other Indian tribes. Then Tecumseh's union might come to pass.

Harrison tried to plant doubts in the minds of the Indians about the Prophet. "If he really is a prophet," Harrison said, "ask him to cause the sun to stand still, the moon to alter its course, the rivers to cease to flow, or the dead to rise from their graves. If he does these things, you may then believe that he has been sent from God."

The Prophet heard about the things that Harrison was saying against him. Perhaps because the Prophet had a bit of the entertainer in him, he decided to take up Harrison's challenge and add to his own reputation while he was at it. A friend had told the Prophet that a total eclipse of the sun would occur at noon on June 16, 1806. He promptly told the Shawnee that on this date, he would command the sun to disappear.

On June 16, a large crowd gathered to see the Prophet make the sun go away. Clothed in a headdress of raven's wings and dark, flowing robes, he looked as if he might be Merlin the magician in King Arthur's court. At the time the eclipse was scheduled to begin, the Prophet looked toward heaven and raised his arms in command. Sure enough, the sky began to darken, and for seven minutes the earth lay in shadow. Then, when the Prophet asked the Great Spirit to bring back the sun, it grew light again. Harrison's plan had backfired. The Shawnee and other Indians present were more impressed than ever by the Prophet. The story of his "miracle" was told to many tribes,

When the Prophet raised his arms skyward, the sun began to darken.

and Indians flocked to the Greenville settlement to see and hear him.

At the same time that the Prophet was gaining in power and influence among Indians, ever greater numbers of white settlers were pouring into the Ohio Valley. Tecumseh believed the time had come to make an all out effort to form an Indian union. But as long as he and the Prophet stayed at the Greenville settlement, Harrison sent spies to watch their every move.

In 1808 Tecumseh asked his brother to move along with his followers to a place in the Indiana Territory that had not been taken by the whites in any treaty. There, near the junction of the Tippecanoe and Wabash rivers, the Prophet established a new settlement that became known as Prophet's Town. In an area far from the nearest white settlement, Harrison found it difficult to keep track of Tecumseh and the Prophet.

For the next four years Tecumseh, along with the Prophet and a few loyal followers, made many long journeys to persuade Indian people to join together in a strong tribal union. He traveled north to the Potawatomi and Winnebago, east to the Wyandot and Iroquois, south to the Creek and Cherokee, and west to the Osage and the Dakota. Everywhere his message was the same—resist the white settlers; save Indian land; live as a free people in a strong and peaceful union. Indians of many tribes responded to his message and pledged their support for his cause.

The translators who have tried to express Tecumseh's words have often given up because they could not come close to the power and beauty of his speech in their own language. A small part of one of his speeches at an Indian council reflects the spirit of his message:

"These lands are ours. No one has a right to remove us, because we were the first owners. The Great Spirit above has appointed this place for us, on which to light our fires, and here we will remain. As to boundaries, the Great Spirit above knows no boundaries, nor will his red people acknowledge any."

Early in his travels Tecumseh gained an ally in the great Potawatomi leader, Shabbona, who pledged the support of his people. Shabbona went with Tecumseh on his journeys and became one of his closest friends. Many of the Winnebago and Wyandot joined Tecumseh's union, even though some of their leaders refused to support it. In the land of the Iroquois Tecumseh did not make many converts, perhaps because the Iroquois and the Shawnee had long been enemies.

After all the successes and failures had been added up, Tecumseh had pledges of support from people in thirty-two tribes. The support came from Indians as far north as the St. Lawrence River, as far south as the Gulf of Mexico, and as far west as the Mississippi Valley.

Governor Harrison heard about the success that Tecumseh had with some of the Indian tribes. Since his strategy was to divide the Indian people and deal with each tribe in treaties, he feared the power of an Indian union. Harrison moved to seize more Indian land while Tecumseh was away seeking the support of Indian tribes. He knew that the Indians at Prophet's Town would not move against him without Tecumseh to lead them. And he wanted to take as much land as possible before Tecumseh's union was strong enough to challenge him.

Harrison quickly gathered a group of Indian chiefs and made them sign the Treaty of Fort Wayne. In this treaty, the United States obtained three million acres of rich land, one hundred miles on both sides of the Wabash River. It was the best game land left in the Ohio Valley. In exchange, the chiefs received some gifts and a large sum of money.

Since 1800, one hundred and ten million acres of Indian land had been taken the same way. Desperate and frightened Indian leaders were bribed and forced into selling the future of their people.

When Tecumseh heard about the Treaty of Fort Wayne, he was heartbroken and angry. He said that the chiefs had no right to sell the land. For Tecumseh and most Indians, land was like air and water. It was freely used by anyone who needed it and could not be sold for any amount of money. Tecumseh demanded that the Americans reject the treaty.

In a letter to Indian leaders, Harrison warned Indian tribes not to join any union against the United States. He warned them that they could not resist the power of white armies. "Our blue coats are more numerous than you can count," Harrison wrote, "and our hunting shirts are like the leaves in the forest or the grains of sand on the Wabash."

Tecumseh was angered by Harrison's threats. He sent a message to Harrison saying that he wanted to tell him how the Shawnee felt about the Treaty of Fort Wayne. In August 1810, Harrison asked Tecumseh to come to Vincennes. It was the first meeting between the two leaders.

CHAPTER VI

Together
We Stand

Tecumseh traveled to the meeting at Vincennes with four hundred armed warriors in eighty canoes along the Wabash River. Harrison had asked Tecumseh to come with only a few of his followers, but Tecumseh wanted to make a show of Indian strength and unity. With him were Wyandot, Kickapoo, Potawatomi, Ottawa, and Winnebago leaders. All the leaders had pledged their support for Tecumseh's union. They were determined to oppose the Treaty of Fort Wayne.

Harrison had arranged to hold the conference on the porch of his home, a mansion built in the style of his native Virginia. With him were the supreme court judges of the Indiana Territory, army officers, and a large group of people from Vincennes.

When Tecumseh stepped ashore, all eyes turned toward him. A U.S. army captain described Tecumseh as "one of the finest looking men I ever saw—about six feet high, straight, with large, fine features, and altogether a daring, bold looking fellow." Tecumseh approached the porch and stopped a short distance from Harrison. Harrison asked Tecumseh to come up on the porch to hold the council.

Tecumseh refused to come onto the porch. He said that

he wanted the meeting to be held in a nearby grove of trees. The reason for this was Tecumseh's strong sense of pride in his people. Indian conferences were held in the open, under the trees or in a clearing. Only white people met on porches. Governor Harrison and his party came down from the porch and put their chairs in the grove.

Tecumseh opened the meeting by asking Harrison to pay close attention to what he had to say. He told him how the whites had driven the Indians from the sea coast and would soon force them far away from their homeland. After he had gone through the long list of broken treaties and promises, he warned that he would do everything in his power to stop further white advances. He condemned the Treaty of Fort Wayne and told Harrison that the Indian people rejected it. Referring to the way that whites made treaties with Indian leaders and tribes rather than with the Indian people as a whole, Tecumseh spoke of his dream of an Indian union.

"Oh, that I might make the fortunes of my red people, and of my country, as great as [my dream], when I think of the Great Spirit that rules this universe! I would not then come to Governor Harrison and ask him to tear up the treaty and [destroy] the landmarks; but I would say to him, 'Sir, you have permission to return to your own country.' . . . Once [my people] were a happy race. Now they are made miserable by the white people who are never contented but always [want more].

"The way, the only way, to check and stop this evil is for all the red men to unite in claiming a common and equal right in the land. That is how it was at first, and should be still, for the land never was divided but belongs to all, for the use of every one. No groups among us have the right to sell, even to one another, much less to strangers who want all and will not do with less."

When Tecumseh spoke of the Indians' "common and equal right to the land," he was speaking of a claim that had been accepted by the United States government shortly after the Revolutionary War. Through the efforts of Joseph Brant, whom Tecumseh had listened to and admired as a child, the American Congress had said that treaties must be made with the Indian people as a whole.

Standing to answer Tecumseh's speech, Harrison defended the treaty of Fort Wayne. He said that the Indian tribes were not all of one nation and that the United States had been just and fair in its dealings with them. To believe that the land was like the air and water, Harrison claimed, was a false idea. According to Harrison, the Indian chiefs who signed the Treaty of Fort Wayne had a right to sell the land, and now the United States owned it.

When Tecumseh heard Harrison say that the United States had been just and fair to the Indian people, he leaped to his feet, shouting "It is false. He lies." Soon all the Indian warriors were on their feet. Some of them made threatening gestures with their tomahawks.

Harrison drew his sword. One of the army officers shouted for the guard to come to defend the whites. For a moment it looked as if there might be fighting. An interpreter told Harrison what Tecumseh had said. Angered, the governor called Tecumseh a bad man and walked out of the meeting, followed by the other whites.

Although the council lasted for two more days, Tecumseh and Harrison did not come any closer to agreement. The

Tecumseh was angered when Harrison said that the Indians had been treated fairly.

Indian leaders who had come with Tecumseh spoke out strongly in favor of an Indian union. They said they would live in peace with the whites only if the Treaty of Fort Wayne was rejected. Unless the Indian land was returned, they said, Tecumseh's union would fight on the side of the British in any future war.

Harrison would not give in. If needed, he said, American soldiers would be used to protect the white settlers on the land given up in the treaty. Harrison, however, was worried about an alliance between the Indian union and the British. At this time many people thought the United States and Great Britain would soon go to war. If a union of Indian tribes supported the British, the Americans might be in deep trouble.

Now more sure than ever that his people would have to go to war with the Americans, Tecumseh moved quickly to gain more support for his Indian union. He went once more to visit the Potawatomi, Ottawa, Winnebago, Sauk, and Fox tribes. At a council at the British Fort Malden in Canada, groups from many Indian tribes came to pledge their aid to his cause.

Late in 1811, Tecumseh journeyed south again to try to convince the southern tribes to join his union. Meeting first with the Choctaw, he told them to "sleep no longer."

"Are we not being stripped day by day of the little that remains of our ancient liberty? Do they not even now kick and strike us as they do their black-faces? How long will it be before they tie us to a post and whip us, and make us work for them in their corn fields as they do them [blacks]? Shall we wait for that moment, or shall we die fighting before submitting to such [slavery]?"

The Choctaw, however, refused to support Tecumseh's cause. They said they would depend on the good will of the United States government and not join the union.

Next Tecumseh spoke to the Creek people at a council attended by five thousand Indians. Silently he led his party of twenty-four warriors into the town square, their faces painted black and their bodies adorned with silver ornaments. At their head Tecumseh walked slowly with a stern look on his face.

Without a word the warriors circled the square three times, scattering their pouches of tobacco and sumac to purify the council grounds. At a signal from Tecumseh, the warriors performed the Shawnee war dance with such grace and power that the onlookers were greatly moved. When

Tecumseh led his party of warriors into the Creek town square where thousands of people had gathered to hear him.

it was over, Tecumseh rose to speak to the thousands who had gathered to hear him.

Sometimes he shouted with a voice like thunder, and at other times he whispered sadly. Tecumseh spoke about the wrongs the whites had committed. Creek land had been stolen, Creek warriors weakened by the white traders' whiskey, Creek women dishonored, and the ashes of the Creek dead stepped on. When Tecumseh finished speaking, a wild war dance broke out among those who listened. But many of the Creek people did not want to join the union. Like the Choctaw, they still trusted the Americans not to push them from their homeland.

Tecumseh and his party went on to the Seminole in what is now Florida, where he won many people to his cause. But the Seminole were not a large tribe, and they were a long way from white settlements.

Turning northward to the Great Smoky Mountains, Tecumseh met in council with the eastern Cherokee, led by Junalaska. There, in the chill mountain air of November, he tried once more to convince Indian people to unite.

"Once our people were many. Once we owned the land from the sunrise to the sunset. Once our campfires twinkled at night like the stars of a fallen sky. Then the white man came. Our campfires dwindled.

"Everywhere our people have passed away, as the snow of the mountains melts in May. We no longer rule the forest. The game has gone like our hunting grounds. Even our lands are nearly gone. Yes, my brothers, our campfires are few. Those that still burn we must draw together.

"Behold what the white man has done to our people! Gone are the Pequot, the Narraganset, the Powhatan, the Tuscarora, and the Coree . . . . Soon there will be no place for the Cherokee to hunt the deer and the bear. The tomahawk of the Shawnee is ready. Will the Cherokee raise the tomahawk? Will the Cherokee join their brothers the Shawnee?"

Many of the young Cherokee warriors shouted "It is true! It is true!" Junalaska, however, spoke to them of the great power of the whites and said that the Cherokee could live in peace with the whites. He persuaded most of the warriors not to follow Tecumseh.

At this point Tecumseh must have been discouraged, but he did not rest. His party journeyed far to the west across the Mississippi to the land of the Osage in the Ozark Mountains. There, also, he failed to gain many new supporters because the Osage had little contact with the whites and could not know the danger they posed. Finally Tecumseh headed back to Prophet's Town.

In six months he had traveled thousands of miles and had spoken to the councils of many tribes, large and small. After all that effort he had no firm pledges of support. He could only hope that when the time came, the people he had spoken to would join with him in their common cause. Unknown to Tecumseh, the time of reckoning had already come for the Indians at Prophet's Town.

As soon as Tecumseh had left on his trip to the southern tribes, Governor Harrison had moved swiftly to gather an army for an attack on the Indian settlement. In September 1811, he marched northward from Vincennes with nearly a thousand soldiers. The army stopped near Prophet's Town to set up camp. Harrison hoped the Indians would attack so he could blame them for the battle.

In Prophet's Town scouts reported all movements of the white army to the Indian leaders. They met in council to decide what to do about the soldiers. Harrison's force had crossed all the treaty lines, and he was clearly bent on destroying Prophet's Town while Tecumseh was away. The Prophet did not believe in violence. He spoke against an attack on the white soldiers. Pressed by the Winnebago leaders, who urged him to order an attack, the Prophet said he would use his powers to protect the Indian warriors.

Just before daylight on a cold, rainy fall day, the Indian forces launched what they thought would be a surprise attack on Harrison's army. Within moments, however,

Harrison's men were on their feet firing at the Indians. When the American cavalry charged, many of the warriors were killed or wounded. Both sides fought hard, but the Indians were outnumbered and lost the battle.

Harrison burned Prophet's Town to the ground and destroyed all the crops. The beautiful village was turned into a wasteland, and the Indian people who lived there fled into the wilderness. They were never again to return.

Tecumseh came back to Prophet's Town several months later. As he walked slowly over the ashes, he must have known that a part of his dream had died with the Indian village.

Harrison was proud of his victory at the town on the Tippecanoe River. Years later, he was elected President of the United States with the slogan "Tippecanoe and Tyler too." But the destruction of Prophet's Town had made the frontier much more dangerous for the settlers. Now the Indians had no place to live. After seeing their homes burned and their crops ruined, they began to attack white settlements to get food and horses.

In June 1812, the United States government declared war on Great Britain. One of the main reasons was to drive the British and the Indians out of the land between the Appalachians and the Mississippi River. Tecumseh saw the war as the last chance for his people. If the Americans won, he believed the Shawnee and many other Indian tribes would be forced from their homelands.

CHAPTER VII

The Last
Battle

Tecumseh gathered all the warriors who would follow him and went to Fort Malden on the Canadian shore of the Detroit River. He pledged his support to the British, who gave his Indian force arms and supplies. As soon as it became known that Tecumseh would lead the Indian forces against the Americans, many Indians flocked to Fort Malden. Among them was the Sauk leader, Black Hawk, and Shabbona with the Potawatomi.

General William Hull was picked to lead the American forces in an attempt to seize Fort Malden. With an army of two thousand men, Hull marched to within a few miles of the British fort. Its only defenders were a small group of British soldiers and Tecumseh's warriors. A British force under Major General Isaac Brock was on the way, but no one knew if they would arrive in time to help defend the fort.

By the time that General Brock and his soldiers arrived at Fort Malden, Tecumseh's men had ambushed part of the American army and forced it to retreat to the fort at Detroit. Brock, the lieutenant governor and army commander of Upper Canada, was a huge, friendly man who was well liked by all who knew him. When he met Tecumseh, the

Tecumseh and General Brock quickly became friends and joined forces for the attack on the fort at Detroit.

two leaders instantly respected each other. Tecumseh said of Brock, "This is a man!" Brock promised Tecumseh that he would help the Indians capture the fort at Detroit and drive the Americans out of their lands.

Together Tecumseh and Brock planned their strategy for the attack on the fort. Tecumseh sketched the rivers and swamps and best approach routes to the area around Detroit. Brock listened carefully. Even though most of his officers said it could not be done, he ordered his men to prepare for an assault on the fort.

When they approached Detroit, Tecumseh used a clever plan to make General Hull believe that he had many more warriors than he did. He had the warriors march in a long column through the woods in full view of the fort. After they had passed from view, the warriors made a quick circle around to the front of the column. Hull looked out of the fort and was frightened to see so many Indians. He did not notice that he was seeing the same Indians making their third and fourth marches past the fort.

Brock and Tecumseh rode together at the head of the British and Indian forces. When they demanded the surrender of the fort, Hull refused. The British guns opened fire, and the bombardment lasted well into the night. At daylight the next day, Tecumseh and Brock were surprised to see a white flag go up over the fort. The Americans in the fort were surprised, too. They wanted to go on fighting.

A British officer rode up to ask about the white flag. General Hull said he was surrendering the fort to the British and Indian forces.

Tecumseh and Brock rode into Detroit and watched the changing of the flags. Brock was so thankful for the help that Tecumseh had given him in the battle that he gave him a beautiful silver sash and a set of fine pistols. Not wanting to keep anything so valuable for himself, Tecumseh gave the gifts to Roundhead, a Wyandot chief. Tecumseh presented Brock with a richly colored wampum belt that had been made for him by the women of Prophet's Town.

A large brick house in Detroit served as headquarters for the two victorious leaders. It was a happy time for Tecumseh, who often walked the streets and talked with the townspeople. In battle Tecumseh was a fierce soldier, but in times of peace he could be a charming friend.

Soon after the surrender of Detroit, Brock had to leave for Niagara to direct the British forces there. Colonel Henry Proctor took command. Proctor was lazy and proud and believed that the Indians were not as good as the British people. From the moment they met, Tecumseh disliked him.

Proctor wanted everyone in Dertoit to take an oath of loyalty to Great Britain. When some of the people refused, he had them put in jail. One of these people was a priest named Father Richard, a well-known French missionary who worked in the churches and schools in Detroit.

Tecumseh knew and respected Father Richard. He went to Proctor and told him the many kind things that the priest had done for the needy Indians around Detroit. Tecumseh demanded that the priest be set free. Proctor refused. Finally, Tecumseh threatened to take all his Indian warriors and leave. This changed Proctor's mind. He set the priest free at once.

One day while Tecumseh was talking to friends on a street corner, a little white girl ran up to him and tugged on his sleeve. She told him that some Indians were stealing from her house.

Tecumseh followed the girl down the street and saw three Indians carrying a trunk out of the house. In a rage Tecumseh attacked the looters. Ashamed and frightened, the warriors dropped the trunk and ran. When Tecumseh went inside the house, he found some British soldiers looking through the family's possessions and angrily threw them out.

That family was not bothered again. Word spread quickly through the town that Tecumseh would not allow looting. And there was no more looting.

In October 1812, Tecumseh learned that his trusted friend, General Isaac Brock, had been killed while leading his men against the Americans at the Niagara border. Deeply saddened by the loss and disgusted by Proctor, Tecumseh left Detroit. When he appeared at Fort Malden in April 1813, he brought with him a force of three thousand warriors! It was the largest Indian force ever assembled to fight against the whites. If the British had a leader equal to Tecumseh, it is possible that their combined forces could have driven the Americans across the Ohio River to the south. But Isaac Brock was gone, and the only officer left to command the British was Colonel Proctor.

In May the British and Indian forces marched south into Ohio to attack the Americans at Fort Meigs. The fort, which was located on the Maumee River near the site of the Battle of Fallen Timbers, had been built under the command of Tecumseh's old enemy, William Henry Harrison. The British and Indian forces surrounded the fort and sent a note to Harrison demanding his surrender. When he refused, the British started bombarding the fort with artillery.

In the battle that followed, Tecumseh planned the strategy and directed most of the fighting. Proctor was a poor leader and spent most of his time safely removed from the action at Fort Miami. He knew little of what was going on and was content to direct his troops from afar.

When American troops sent to help defend the fort landed on the north bank of the Maumee, Tecumseh set a trap for them. An advance guard of Tecumseh's warriors attacked briefly and then disappeared into the woods. The Americans chased Tecumseh's warriors far into the forest. Suddenly the Indians stopped and turned to face the Americans. The soldiers paused for a moment, and before they knew it, Tecumseh's main force had surrounded them. Desperately the Americans tried to retreat to the river, but many of them fell in the deadly fire and the hand-to-hand fighting that followed. Only a few of the men made it back to the fort. The rest of them had fallen in the battle or were taken prisoner.

After the battle the American prisoners were taken to Fort Miami and left in charge of Proctor. Tecumseh was on the way back to Fort Meigs when a Shawnee came running through the forest after him. The Shawnee said the prisoners were being killed by some of the Indian warriors.

Enraged, Tecumseh spun around on his horse and rushed back to Fort Miami. Charging into the fort, Tecumseh

When he heard about the killing of prisoners, Tecumseh charged into the fort to stop the warriors who had disobeyed him.

shouted in a thunderous voice for the killing to stop. He saw two warriors about to kill a prisoner and leaped off his horse at them. Grabbing both warriors by the throat, Tecumseh threw them to the ground. He drew his tomahawk and ran between the Indians and the prisoners. The Indians fell back and ran away.

Tears ran down Tecumseh's face. The Indians had forgotten his orders to treat the prisoners well. They remembered all the wrongs they had suffered at the hands of the whites, and this had driven them to a terrible revenge. Tecumseh saw Proctor sitting nearby. He demanded to know why Proctor had let the killing go on. Proctor answered that Indians could not be commanded. Tecumseh shouted "Begone! You are unfit to command. I came to save, you to murder."

A few days after Tecumseh's victory near Fort Meigs, Proctor decided to lift the seige on the fort and return to Fort Malden. Tecumseh was furious, but he had no choice than to go along with the British. By themselves the Indians who fought with him were not strong enough to defeat the Americans.

The British and Indian forces at Fort Malden were supplied by the British Navy, which controlled the shipping routes on Lake Erie. In September 1813, an American fleet under Commodore Oliver Perry defeated the British and cut off the supply route to Fort Malden. At the same time an American army commanded by William Henry Harrison was advancing toward Fort Malden from the south.

Proctor said that Fort Malden could no longer be defended. Tecumseh disagreed. In a stirring speech to the Indians and British at the fort, he called for Proctor to stand

Commodore Oliver Perry defeated the British fleet on Lake Erie. With their supply line cut off, the British and Indian forces had to retreat into Canada.

and fight. Proctor would not, even though most of his officers wanted to defend the fort. He ordered a retreat eastward along the Thames River.

At a place near Moraviantown where fertile farmland bounded the river, Tecumseh shamed Proctor into making a stand against Harrison's army. That night Tecumseh had a vision of his death in the battle to come. He spent the night with Shabbona and others in his group of close friends who had followed him over the years. "Brother warriors," he said, "We are about to enter an engagement from which I shall not return. My body will remain on the field of battle."

On the morning of October 5, 1813, Tecumseh shook hands with all the British soldiers, telling each one of them to "be brave, stand firm, shoot straight." Proctor was not interested in fighting that hard. At the first charge of the American cavalry, he ran to the rear, jumped on a fast horse, and galloped away.

During the battle Tecumseh stood in the midst of the fighting and rallied his warriors again and again. Long after the British had surrendered, the Indians fought on. Greatly outnumbered by the soldiers, they would not give up. They all seemed to know that everything depended on this battle. If they lost here, they would lose forever.

Though Tecumseh was shot in the arm and the chest, he shouted for the warriors to keep fighting. Finally the Indian warriors heard his voice no more. The battle was over.

The Battle of the Thames broke the power of the Indian people of the Ohio Valley. By that winter all the land was under the control of the white settlers.

In the 1820s the Shawnee people whom Tecumseh had

loved so deeply were moved west to a narrow strip of land south of the Kansas River. One by one, all the tribes of the Ohio Valley were forced from their homelands. Gone were the swift-moving rivers and the plentiful fruit and game. Gone were the green forests. And gone was the Chief of the Beautiful River.

After his death many legends grew up about Tecumseh. One legend says that his powerful voice can still be heard in the autumn at sunset calling to the Indian people. The voice calls out to remind the people of their greatness. It may be hoped that the Indians living in America today remember with pride this great man who so loved his people that he died for them.

THE AUTHOR

As a social studies teacher and chairperson
of the social science department of the
Academy of Our Lady of Peace in San
Diego, California, Anne Schraff has long
been interested in young people. She has
written many articles and books for young
readers and is currently on leave from
her teaching duties to devote more time
to writing. A *magna cum laude* graduate
of California State University, she also
holds a Master's degree in American
history and is a member of the California
Council on Social Studies.

*Photos reproduced through the courtesy
of the American Museum of Natural
History, the Indiana Historical Society
Library, the Library of Congress, the Lick
Observatory, the Ohio Historical Society,
and the Smithsonian Institution,
Anthropological Archives.*

OTHER BIOGRAPHIES
IN THIS SERIES ARE

William Beltz
Robert Bennett
Black Hawk
Crazy Horse
Geronimo
Oscar Howe
Pauline Johnson
Chief Joseph
Little Turtle
Maria Martinez
George Morrison
Daisy Hooee Nampeyo
Michael Naranjo
Osceola
Powhatan
Red Cloud
Sacagawea
Sealth
Sequoyah
Sitting Bull
Maria Tallchief
Jim Thorpe
Tomo-chi-chi
Pablita Velarde
William Warren
Annie Wauneka